EYE ON ENERGY
Alternative Cars

ABDO
Publishing Company

Jill C. Wheeler

visit us at
www.abdopublishing.com

Published by ABDO Publishing Company, 8000 West 78th Street, Edina, Minnesota 55439. Copyright © 2008 by Abdo Consulting Group, Inc. International copyrights reserved in all countries. No part of this book may be reproduced in any form without written permission from the publisher. The Checkerboard Library™ is a trademark and logo of ABDO Publishing Company.

Printed in the United States.

Cover Photo: Corbis
Interior Photos: Alamy pp. 14, 16, 24; AP Images pp. 8, 9, 10, 15, 19, 21, 22, 27; Corbis pp. 4, 5, 13, 25, 28, 29; Getty Images pp. 7, 13, 17, 20, 23; Peter Arnold p. 6; Wire Image p. 11

Series Coordinator: Rochelle Baltzer
Editors: Rochelle Baltzer, BreAnn Rumsch
Art Direction & Cover Design: Neil Klinepier

Library of Congress Cataloging-in-Publication Data

Wheeler, Jill C., 1964-
  Alternative cars / Jill C. Wheeler.
    p. cm. – (Eye on energy)
  Includes index.
  ISBN 978–1–59928–803–1
  1. Alternative fuel vehicles–Juvenile literature. I. Title.

TL216.5.W485 2008
629.22'9–dc22
                                                    2007007107

CONTENTS

CARS EVERYWHERE

Americans have driven cars for more than 100 years. Throughout this time, cars have become a major part of the American lifestyle. Most U.S. families own at least one car. This may be due to the limited mass-**transit** options in many parts of the country. And in some places, weather conditions make walking or bicycling year-round difficult.

There are 136 million passenger cars in the United States. About 97 percent of them rely on the internal **combustion** engine (ICE). ICE cars and trucks use 50 to 70 percent of oil produced in the country. They use so much because their engines are **inefficient**.

In the 1950s and 1960s, more families became able to afford one or two automobiles. This encouraged them to move to suburbs and commute to cities for work.

But, the engine isn't the only problem. Some people prefer fast sports cars, heavy, powerful trucks, or sport-utility vehicles (SUVs). Moving fast or pulling heavy weight uses additional fuel. So, these powerful vehicles are even more **inefficient**. Automakers say they would build more efficient vehicles if they knew that more people would buy them.

The United States has about 25 percent of the world's passenger cars. About 80 percent of U.S. households own a car.

ENERGY BUZZ
Transportation accounts for more than one-fourth of the energy used in the United States.

When fuel is inexpensive, fuel **efficiency** is not a major concern for most drivers. However, fuel prices have increased in recent years. This is partly because the United States largely depends on imported oil. Yet, much of the world's oil is located in politically unstable countries. So, the United States may not always be able to obtain the amount of oil it currently consumes.

In addition, ICE vehicles cause **environmental** problems. Their **exhaust** contains unburned or partially burned fuels. These **emissions** are poisonous and contribute to smog. ICE vehicles also emit other harmful gases.

For these reasons, consumers and car companies have shown interest in alternative cars. Some alternatives, such as electric cars, have been around for many years. Others, such as hydrogen fuel-cell cars, are still being developed. Despite their differences, alternative cars share a common goal. They provide more efficient transportation with less harmful effects.

Smog blankets Los Angeles, California. This pollution can reduce visibility, damage plants, irritate eyes, and cause breathing problems.

HOW FAR PER GALLON?

When gasoline prices rise, many people pay closer attention to the fuel economy of their vehicles. Fuel economy is measured by how many miles a vehicle can travel using one gallon (4 L) of fuel.

The U.S. government publishes a list of fuel economy ratings for cars. However, many drivers report that they get fewer miles per gallon than the listed amount. This is because the rating system does not reflect how most people drive.

Fuel economy ratings assume people drive no more than 60 miles per hour (97 km/h). And, they assume people accelerate slowly, going from 0 to 60 miles per hour in 18 seconds. However, the average driver accelerates about five times as quickly.

Weather also affects fuel economy. Federal standards measure fuel economy at 68 to 86 degrees Fahrenheit (20 to 30°C), without air conditioning. In most places, temperatures are well outside that range.

Finally, more energy is needed to move heavy weight. Today, the average U.S. adult weighs about 25 pounds (11 kg) more than the average adult in 1960. Compared to the yearly amount of gasoline that U.S. passenger vehicles burned in 1960, they burn an additional 938 million gallons (4 billion L) today. That extra gasoline would be enough to fuel nearly 2 million cars for a year!

ConocoPhillips

Regular Gasoline	365 9/10
Plus Gasoline	385 9/10
Premium Gasoline	395 9/10
Diesel #2	297 9/10

Racing Fuel

Food Mart

An average gasoline-fueled passenger car uses 581 gallons (2,199 L) of gasoline every year. An average light truck uses 813 gallons (3,078 L).

ELECTRIC CARS

Electric cars were first used in the late 1880s. They competed with gasoline-powered ICE cars. Some people preferred electric cars because they were quiet, easy to operate, and did not release smelly **emissions**. In 1900, 38 percent of U.S. cars produced were electric.

In the early 1900s, electric cars could not travel very fast or very far. But that didn't stop them from becoming popular, especially in cities.

Yet, electric cars had some major disadvantages. They were limited in travel distance and speed. Plus, they were costlier than ICE cars. Electric cars lost popularity after mass-produced ICE cars, such as the Ford Model T, hit the roads. By the late 1920s, electric cars were nearly gone. ICE cars had become the favorite.

However, electric cars made comebacks in later years. In the 1960s, America experienced a decrease in the **petroleum** supply. And, many people became concerned about pollution. These issues renewed an interest in electric cars.

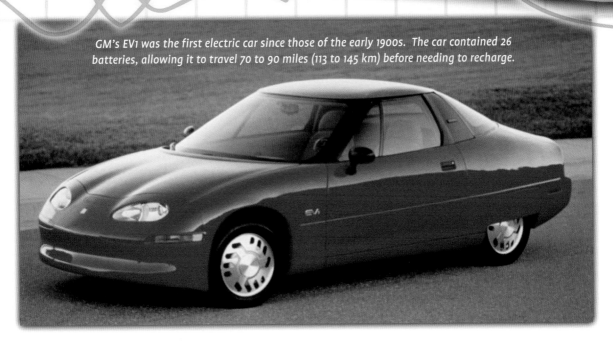

GM's EV1 was the first electric car since those of the early 1900s. The car contained 26 batteries, allowing it to travel 70 to 90 miles (113 to 145 km) before needing to recharge.

Californians in particular worried about smog and pollution. They knew they wouldn't be able to clean up pollution if they did not drive cleaner cars. So, they wanted vehicles that produced no **emissions**. In 1990, the state passed a law that required some cars on California roads to have no emissions. In 1996, General Motors Corporation (GM) responded by creating the EV1 electric car.

FACT OR FICTION?

Los Angeles, California, produces more pollutants than any other U.S. city.

Fiction. New York City, New York, actually produces more. But because of its landscape and cooler climate, New York City has less of an air-pollution problem than Los Angeles.

GM built 1,117 EV1s between 1996 and 1999. The cars were **leased** only in California and Arizona. EV1s made nearly no noise, and most drivers loved them. After driving the cars, people plugged them in to recharge. EV1s took eight hours or fewer to fully recharge.

EV1 drivers could recharge their cars at various places, including shopping malls, parks, and hotels.

However, GM cancelled the EV1 program in 2004. The company said that not enough consumers wanted the cars, which made them unprofitable. GM took back the cars and destroyed most of them. This angered many people. Some people believed GM gave in to pressure from the oil industry. Oil companies did not want electric cars to succeed because they would lose money in gasoline sales.

In July 2006, Tesla Motors unveiled a new electric car called the Tesla Roadster. The Roadster is so popular that there is a long waiting list to purchase one. Like the EV1, it has no **emissions**. It can travel about 250 miles (400 km) per charge. And, it has just one moving part. So, there is less weight to support and fewer parts to wear down or break.

Yet, there are downsides to electric cars. Charging an electric car still requires electricity to be generated. Electricity is usually produced from **fossil fuels** such as coal. Burning these fuels adds to **global warming**. Also, it is not yet known how long electric car batteries can last. Over time, all batteries slowly lose effectiveness.

The Tesla Roadster is produced in limited numbers. And, it is expensive. In 2007, it had a base price of $92,000.

Better Batteries

Producing batteries remains the biggest hurdle in the creation of electric cars. An electric-car battery must be able to deliver power for a long time without wearing down. And, it needs to be 2,000 times as powerful as a laptop computer battery. Yet, building a battery with such power can be difficult because of size. The more energy stored in a small battery, the more dangerous it becomes.

Some laptop computer batteries have proven this point. In recent years, computer companies took back laptop batteries from consumers because of manufacturing errors. Chemicals packed inside of the small batteries might have caused fires.

If electric cars are to become popular transportation options, battery technology must improve. So, researchers are developing better electric-car batteries. However, these batteries are expensive to build. Yet the more demand there is for such batteries, the cheaper the batteries will be to produce.

Consumers and lawmakers must speak up if they want electric cars. Car companies will not spend money to build them unless they know the cars can be sold. And, oil companies will continue to support gasoline-powered cars or gasoline-electric hybrids rather than electric cars. These companies spend billions of dollars to find, **refine**, and transport oil. They will lose money if many people switch to electric cars.

Under the hood of a ZAP L.U.V.

In 2003, an electric vehicle company called Zero Air Pollution (ZAP) announced a breakthrough in battery technology that could quadruple the range of electric vehicles. ZAP applied the technology to its Light Utility Vehicle (L.U.V.).

HYBRID CARS

A hybrid car uses two types of power systems. One of today's most popular alternative cars is the gasoline-electric hybrid. This car has a gasoline-powered ICE and a battery-powered electric motor. The gasoline-electric hybrid is designed to travel more miles per gallon of fuel with less **emissions** than standard ICE cars.

Most hybrid cars charge their batteries by regenerative braking. In this process, the motor captures energy from the car's forward motion during braking. This energy charges the battery.

In stop-and-go traffic, gasoline-electric hybrids run on only their electric motors. The constant braking recharges the battery, so the car does not need to use the ICE. When using the electric motor,

no **greenhouse gases** are emitted. On highways or when traveling faster, gasoline-electric hybrids use their ICEs.

Hybrid cars are ideal for driving on busy city streets. They are claimed to get 25 percent better fuel economy than standard ICE cars.

Gasoline-electric hybrids have gained interest and popularity in recent years, but the idea is not new. In 1904, American engineer H. Piper invented the hybrid-car concept. His idea was initially unsuccessful, partly because of high development costs.

A gasoline engine (left) and an electric power system (right) work together in a Toyota Prius. The Prius was rated one of the greenest, or most environmentally friendly, cars in 2007.

Hybrid technology continued to develop over the years. Yet, it was not widely applied to cars. In fact, it was first used for trains. The diesel-electric engine proved to be the most practical option for trains, which is still true today. Diesel-electric engines are also made for mass-**transit** buses.

Most of today's locomotives are diesel-electric hybrids.

The first mass-produced gasoline-electric hybrid car was the Toyota Prius. The Prius became available for sale in 1997 in Japan. By 2001, the car was available worldwide. Other hybrids have since become mass produced. Frequently, hybrid cars are so popular that there are waiting lists to purchase one.

Despite their increasing popularity, gasoline-electric hybrid cars have some disadvantages. They are more expensive than standard ICE cars. Also, some critics argue that they do not get the fuel economy they are promoted to get. Plus, gasoline-electric hybrids still burn gasoline and **emit greenhouse gases** when using the ICE.

Automakers are also building gasoline-electric hybrid vehicles that can be plugged into electrical outlets. These plug-in hybrids can travel more miles using electricity than hybrids recharged by regenerative braking. That means they burn less gasoline.

Still, plug-in hybrids have drawbacks. A majority of the electricity produced in the United States comes from coal. So, coal has most likely produced the electricity gained from an electrical outlet. That means plug-in hybrids fundamentally contribute to **global warming**.

Hybrid-car owners enjoy several perks. Some states allow hybrid cars to drive in highway lanes normally reserved for buses or carpools. Certain states also offer tax paybacks to these drivers.

HYDRAULIC ENERGY

Gasoline-electric hybrid cars cost more than conventional ICE cars. This is because they require a large, heavy battery. Yet, there are other hybrids that use no battery at all.

Instead of storing energy in a battery, hydraulic hybrids store it in pressurized tanks. When braking, energy from the wheels pumps fluid into a tank that holds **nitrogen**. The fluid compresses the gas to about 5,000 pounds per square inch (350 kg/sq cm). That pressure forces fluid through a pump, which drives the wheels.

This technology works best for large vehicles that stop and start a lot. Delivery trucks and garbage trucks are ideal for a hydraulic hybrid system. Researchers think vehicles the size of SUVs might be able to use this type of system, too.

Hydraulic hybrids have several advantages. Since they do not contain large batteries, they are easier to maintain. Plus, the pressurized tanks can accept and deliver large amounts of power quickly. For example, one hydraulic hybrid van can deliver 100 **horsepower** for about 20 seconds. No electric battery could absorb and deliver that much power so quickly.

But, there are also disadvantages to hydraulic hybrids. Their storage tanks are large and bulky. And like other hybrids, they still use some gasoline or diesel fuel. The hydraulic part of the engine only works when stopping and starting. So during highway driving, either gasoline or diesel fuel is burned. Those fuels **emit greenhouse gases** and other pollutants.

The truck's hydraulic system can capture and store a large amount of the energy that is normally wasted when braking.

The U.S. Environmental Protection Agency and the United Parcel Service (UPS) of America partnered to make a hydraulic hybrid UPS delivery truck. The truck has a fuel economy improvement of 60 to 70 percent, as well as a 40 percent reduction in greenhouse gas emissions.

DIESEL CARS

Diesel cars use diesel fuel instead of gasoline. Diesel fuel contains more energy than gasoline. And, engines can more **efficiently** burn diesel fuel than gasoline. In fact, diesel engines can get up to 40 percent greater fuel economy than comparable gasoline engines. They **emit** about one-third less **greenhouse gases** than most gasoline engines, too!

Diesel fuel is widely used to power school and public buses in the United States.

Despite these benefits, traditional diesel cars emit more smog-forming pollutants than gasoline-powered cars. In fact, diesel vehicles are responsible for almost half of all harmful **nitrogen** oxides produced by U.S. cars and trucks. They are responsible for more than two-thirds of all **soot**, too.

However, researchers have found ways to make diesel vehicles cleaner.

Since October 2006, ultra-low sulfur diesel (ULSD) has been available throughout the United States. ULSD contains just 3 percent of the sulfur of regular diesel fuel. Diesel engines are also becoming even more **efficient**.

Biodiesel is another option. This fuel is made from specially treated **renewable** resources, such as soybeans or canola seeds. Sometimes, biodiesel is used alone. Other times, it is mixed with regular diesel fuel. Either way, biodiesel **emits** fewer pollutants and particles than regular diesel fuel. But, it is not yet widely available.

In the United States, most biodiesel is made from soybean oil. But, some producers make the fuel from palm oil, animal fats, or recycled oils.

It is estimated that the number of diesel cars in the United States will triple in the next ten years. Many people are excited about these new, cleaner vehicles. The improved fuel efficiency of diesel cars could help reduce U.S. dependency on foreign oil.

HYDROGEN POWER

Some people believe that one day hydrogen will become the primary energy source in the United States. Hydrogen is the most abundant **element** in the universe. In fact, about 90 percent of the universe's atoms are hydrogen! Hydrogen is usually found in gas form, but it can combine with other elements to make different things. For example, hydrogen and oxygen makes water.

Most researchers believe hydrogen's best **potential** for energy is to be used as fuel in a fuel cell. A fuel cell is different from a battery. Batteries hold energy and must be recharged when that energy is gone. But, fuel cells continuously convert chemical energy into electrical energy. So, they can supply electrical energy for a much longer time than a battery can.

The first fuel cell was developed in 1843. Since then, they have been used for space exploration. Fuel cells have also been used as back-up power sources for hospitals,

Hydrogen fuel-cell batteries power the electrical systems in space shuttles. And, liquid hydrogen is used as fuel to lift shuttles into orbit.

universities, and office buildings. More recently, fuel-cell technology has been applied to cars.

Hydrogen fuel-cell cars are electric cars that use fuel cells instead of batteries for power. They **emit** only heat and minimal water vapor. Personal fuel-cell vehicles were first sold in 2004 in Germany. By November 2006, there were about 500 hydrogen-powered cars in use throughout the world.

In January 2007, Ford Motor Company unveiled the world's first drivable fuel-cell hybrid car. The car combines a hydrogen fuel-cell generator with batteries. It can be plugged in to recharge the batteries.

Most experts believe it will be many years before hydrogen fuel-cell cars are popular. The cars are very expensive to build, which makes them expensive to purchase. They can cost close to $1 million to construct. Those costs must decrease before many people will buy them.

In the United States in 2006, there were about 25 hydrogen fueling stations and 200 hydrogen-fueled vehicles.

Currently, there are very few hydrogen fueling stations. And, energy companies will not build more fueling stations if the fuel-cell car **market** is not in demand.

Some people do not want such stations near their homes for fear of explosions. Hydrogen catches fire easily. And it is very light, so it is packed in containers under high pressure. There could be dangerous explosions if the containers were ever broken. Yet, other people say hydrogen is no more dangerous than other flammable fuels, including gasoline.

Hydrogen fuel-cell technology for cars is meant to be an **environmentally** friendly option. However, turning natural hydrogen into hydrogen for fuel requires a lot of energy. If that energy is supplied by power plants that burn **fossil fuels**, the use of hydrogen fuel cells still causes **greenhouse gas emissions**.

PROJECT DRIVEWAY

In fall 2007, 100 hydrogen fuel-cell vehicles hit the roads in New York City, Washington, D.C., and three regions of California.

VEHICLE: The four-seat, front-wheel drive Chevrolet Equinox fuel-cell vehicle (FCV) is being used for the test.

TIMELINE: The test will run between 3 and 30 months. GM will decide by December 31, 2009, whether to proceed with hydrogen fuel-cell vehicle production.

Project Driveway represents the first major market test of fuel-cell vehicles in the United States.

TECHNOLOGY: The Equinox FCV is powered by a fuel cell, which operates in temperatures between 13 and 113 degrees Fahrenheit (-11 and 45°C). Three storage tanks hold 9.2 pounds (4.2 kg) of hydrogen. A battery pack supplements the fuel cell and captures energy from regenerative braking.

SPEED AND RANGE: The Equinox FCV has a top speed of 100 miles per hour (160 km/h). It can go from 0 to 60 miles per hour (0 to 97 km/h) in 12 seconds. And, it can drive 200 miles (320 km) per tank of fuel. A tank stores up to 9.26 pounds (4.2 kg) of hydrogen gas under high pressure.

HIGHLIGHTS: The Equinox FCV is a zero-emissions vehicle. Water vapor is the only substance emitted. There are four water vapor outlets at the rear of the car.

OTHER FUELS

Natural gas and gasoline-**ethanol** blends have been sources of energy for many years. Recently, growing interest in alternative cars has emphasized these fuels. In addition, using natural gas and ethanol helps the United States depend less on foreign oil.

Worldwide, there are more than 5 million vehicles powered by natural gas. More than 150,000 of them are on U.S. roadways. Most of them are fleet vehicles, such as city buses, which refuel at the same place. Fleet vehicles are ideal for this technology since there are few natural gas stations available to the general public.

Natural-gas vehicles **emit** less **greenhouse gases** than traditional gasoline- and diesel-powered vehicles. And unlike diesel vehicles, they do not emit other smog-forming pollutants. However, they cost more than gasoline-fueled vehicles. And, natural-gas vehicles have a shorter driving range. This is partly because natural gas contains less energy than gasoline.

In the United States, ethanol blends are becoming increasingly popular as fuel. There are more than 6 million flex-fuel vehicles on U.S. roads. These vehicles can run on E85, a mixture of 15 percent gasoline and 85 percent ethanol.

Most **ethanol** in the United States is made from corn, a **renewable** resource. Ethanol contains less energy than gasoline, yet more energy than natural gas. And, E85-fueled vehicles **emit** less **greenhouse gases** than traditional gasoline-powered vehicles.

Corn is processed into ethanol at an ethanol plant. Because of its abundance and low price, corn is the main resource for producing ethanol in the United States.

GOING GREEN

Most people think of improved fuel **efficiency** and less **emissions** when they think of alternative cars. But, some automakers are also planning ways to make the rest of the car more **environmentally** friendly.

Already, some cars around the world have floor mats and spare-tire covers made of bioplastics. Bioplastics are plasticlike materials made from plants instead of **petroleum**. These materials are considered "carbon neutral." That means the plants absorb as much **carbon dioxide** while growing as they release when turned into plastics.

Some automakers are also researching how to use plant-based materials instead of metals and plastics for car exteriors. One company is studying how to make car hoods and roofs from kenaf. Kenaf is a fast-growing plant that absorbs carbon dioxide quickly.

Leading producers of kenaf are India, Thailand, and China.

Another company has made car panels from bamboo fiber, sugar cane, and corn. Yet another company is looking to use corn to make fabric for interior car parts, such as seats.

Making car parts from plants is more expensive than using steel and oil. However, that may change as the price of oil continues to rise. Eventually, **environmentally** friendly cars may be more affordable for more people. And as alternative engines and fuels continue to develop, alternative cars will likely be the transportation of the future.

Toyota Motor Corporation created the i-unit from plant-based materials, such as kenaf. Upright, the personal vehicle is 3 feet (1 m) wide and 6 feet (2 m) tall. It reclines into a sports-car position to travel at speeds of up to 25 miles per hour (40 km/h).

GLOSSARY

carbon dioxide - a heavy, fireproof, colorless gas that is formed when fuel containing the element carbon is burned.

combustion - the act or instance of burning.

efficient - the ability to produce a desired result, especially without wasting time or energy. Something that is wasteful of time or energy is inefficient.

element - any of the more than 100 basic substances that have atoms of only one kind.

emit - to give off or out. An emission is something that has been emitted.

environmental - of or having to do with all the surroundings that affect the growth and well-being of a living thing.

ethanol - a colorless, flammable liquid that is used in liquors and fuel.

exhaust - used gas or vapor that escapes from an engine.

fossil fuel - a fuel that is formed in the earth from the remains of plants or animals. Coal, oil, and natural gas are fossil fuels.

global warming - an increase in the average temperature of Earth's surface.

greenhouse gas - a gas, such as carbon dioxide, that traps heat in the atmosphere.

horsepower - a unit for measuring the power of an engine or a motor. One horsepower is equal to the power it takes to lift 550 pounds (250 kg) one foot, or 12 inches (30 cm), in one second.

lease - to grant usage by a contract by which a person conveys real estate, equipment, or facilities for a specific time and price.

market - the opportunity for selling.

nitrogen - a colorless, odorless, tasteless gas that is the most plentiful element in Earth's atmosphere and is found in all living matter. Nitrogen oxide is any of several compounds of nitrogen and oxygen. It is considered a pollutant of the atmosphere.

petroleum - a thick, dark-colored liquid that is a fossil fuel. It can be refined to make fuel and other products, such as plastics, fertilizers, and drugs.

potential - capable of being or becoming. Something that is possible, but not actual.

refine - to purify. A refinery is the building and the machinery for purifying products, such as petroleum.

renewable - able to replenish naturally in a relatively short period of time. Renewable energy resources include biomass, hydropower, geothermal energy, wind energy, and solar energy.

soot - a black substance in the smoke from burning coal, wood, oil, or other fuel.

transit - the moving of persons or things from one place to another.

WEB SITES

To learn more about alternative cars, visit ABDO Publishing Company on the World Wide Web at **www.abdopublishing.com**. Web sites about alternative cars are featured on our Book Links page. These links are routinely monitored and updated to provide the most current information available.

INDEX

B
batteries 11, 12, 14, 18, 22, 23
biodiesel 21
bioplastics 28

C
carbon dioxide 28

D
diesel fuel 16, 19, 20, 21, 26

E
E85 26, 27
electricity 6, 8, 9, 10, 11, 12, 13, 14, 15, 16, 17, 18, 22, 23
ethanol 26, 27

F
Ford Model T 8
fossil fuels 4, 6, 8, 10, 11, 12, 13, 17, 21, 24, 26, 27, 28, 29
fuel cell 6, 22, 23, 24
fuel economy 14, 16, 20

fuel efficiency 4, 5, 6, 20, 21, 28

G
gasoline 8, 10, 13, 14, 15, 16, 18, 19, 20, 24, 26, 27
General Motors Corporation EV1 9, 10
Germany 23
global warming 11, 17
greenhouse gases 14, 16, 19, 20, 24, 26, 27

H
hybrids 13, 14, 15, 16, 17, 18, 19
hydrogen 6, 22, 23, 24

I
importing 6
internal combustion engine 4, 5, 6, 8, 14, 16, 18

J
Japan 16

M
mass transit 4, 16, 26

N
nitrogen 18, 20

P
Piper, H. 15
pollution 6, 8, 9, 14, 19, 20, 21, 24, 26, 28

S
sulfur 21

T
Tesla Roadster 10
Toyota Prius 16

U
ultra-low sulfur diesel 21
United States 4, 6, 8, 9, 10, 15, 17, 20, 21, 22, 26, 27